MAMBAS

THE SNAKE DISCOVERY LIBRARY

Sherie Bargar   Linda Johnson

Photographer/Consultant: George Van Horn

Watermill Press

Mahwah, New Jersey

Library of Congress Cataloging in Publication Data

Bargar, Sherie, 1944-
    Discover Mambas.

    (Snake discovery library)
    Includes index.
    Summary: An introduction to the physical character-
istics, habits, natural environment and relationship
to human beings of the various species of mambas.
    1. Mambas—Juvenile literature.   [1. Mambas.
2. Poisonous snakes.   3. Snakes]   I. Johnson,
Linda, 1947-   .   II. Van Horn, George, ill.
III. Title.   IV. Series: Bargar, Sherie, 1944-
Snake discovery library.
QL666.064B373   1986   597.96   86-17707
ISBN 0-86592-960-2

Title Photo:
East African Green Mamba
Dendroaspis angusticeps

TABLE OF CONTENTS

Mambas   5
Where They Live   6
How They Look   9
Their Senses   11
The Head and Mouth   14
Baby Mambas   16
Prey   19
Their Defense   20
Mambas and People   22
Glossary   23
Index   24

MAMBAS

The Jameson's Mamba, Black Mamba, and the 2 species of Green Mambas are members of the *Elapid* family. People fear the famous African mamba more than any other snake because of its **poisonous** bite. The fast and agile mamba may travel up to 7 miles per hour. The Black Mamba can move with its head and front part of its body above the ground.

Black Mamba
Dendroaspis polylepis

WHERE THEY LIVE

Trees and bushes of the African **savannahs** are the homes of Green Mambas. The tree dwelling Green Mambas are masters of gliding gracefully through branches. The Jameson's Mamba lives in the trees of Central Africa. Rocks, tall grasses, burrows of other animals, and the forest floor are the homes of the Black Mamba. Termite mounds are a favorite home and nesting place of the Black Mamba.

Jameson's Mamba
Dendroaspis jamesoni

HOW THEY LOOK

Mambas have smooth scales and slender, muscular bodies. Green mambas which grow to 6 or 7 feet are combinations of green, yellow, and black. The West African Green Mamba has large green scales bordered by black skin. The scales become a golden yellow toward the tail making this one of the most beautiful of all tree snakes. Black Mambas which grow to 14 feet are actually brown or grey.

Jameson's Mamba
Dendroaspis jamesoni

THEIR SENSES

The mamba's sight and taste determine the size and location of its **prey**. Its large eyes see **prey** better than most snakes. As it approaches **prey**, the Jacobson's organ in the roof of its mouth **analyzes** the particles brought to it by the tongue. Once the Jacobson's organ has confirmed that **prey** is near, the mamba follows the **prey** for the kill.

Black Mamba
Dendroaspis polylepis

RUFFNER SCHOOL

Jameson's Mamba
Dendroaspis jamesoni

THE HEAD AND MOUTH

The tapered snout on the slender head of the mamba improves its **depth perception**. Hollow fangs are at the front of the upper jaw. During the bite, the muscles around the **venon** glands pump the **venom** through the fangs and into the **prey**. The jaws stretch like a rubber band to swallow whole animals. The windpipe extends from the throat to the front of the mouth and lets the snake breathe while swallowing **prey**.

West African Green Mamba
Dendroaspis viridis

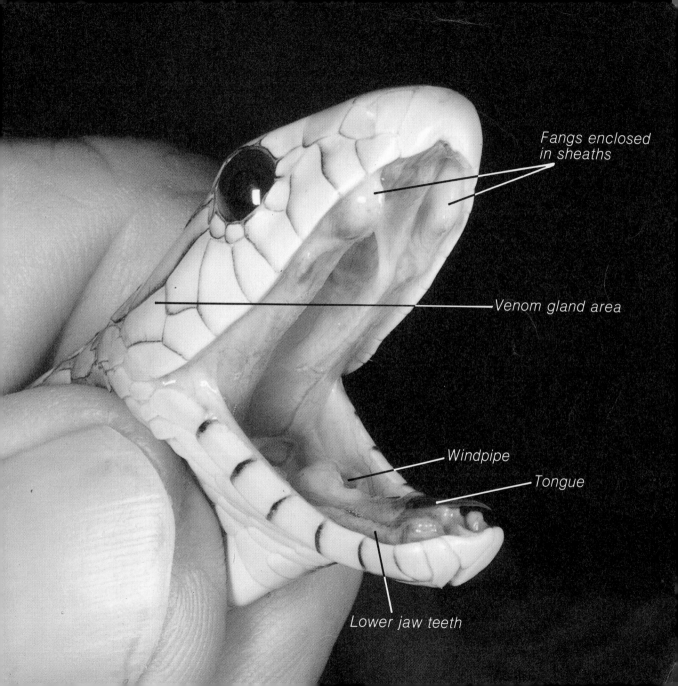

Fangs enclosed in sheaths

Venom gland area

Windpipe

Tongue

Lower jaw teeth

BABY MAMBAS

Female mambas like to lay their eggs in damp decaying vegetation on the forest floor. In spring or early summer 9 to 14 baby mambas **pip** their leathery eggs with the **egg tooth**. The 15 to 24 inch babies weigh about 1 ounce and take care of themselves from birth. Black Mambas grow an amazing 4½ feet in their first year of life and increase their birth weight as much as 100 times.

PREY

Birds, squirrels, mice, and rats are eaten by mambas. The mamba's quick deadly strike reaches almost half of its body length. The Green Mamba watches for its **prey** to move within striking distance. It aims its bite for the back of the neck and rarely releases it. Because the Green Mamba lives in trees, it cannot afford to let the **prey** fall to the ground.

West African Green Mamba
Dendroaspis viridis

THEIR DEFENSE

Camouflaged by leaves and branches, the Green Mamba is protected from most enemies. Black Mambas hide from enemies in burrows, tree stumps, and rock crevices. When escape is impossible and the mamba is cornered by an enemy, it raises its head and flattens its neck. If the enemy moves too close, the mamba will not hesitate to bite.

Black Mamba
Dendroaspis polylepis

MAMBAS AND PEOPLE

The shy mamba is seldom seen and will flee from humans when possible. When cornered the shy mamba will fight fiercely. Experts estimate 2 drops of Black Mamba **venom** can kill a human. No one has survived a mamba bite without prompt medical treatment. The mamba's life threatening **venom** may help humans by unlocking the secrets of the human brain.

GLOSSARY

agile (AG ile) — Easy and quick moving.

analyze (AN a lyze) analyzes — To find out what something is.

depth perception (DEPTH per CEP tion) — The ability to determine distance using the vision of both eyes focusing on the same object.

egg tooth (EGG TOOTH) — A temporary tiny ridge which is very sharp and used to open the egg. It is on the tip of a baby snake's nose.

pip (PIP) — The first opening made by an animal hatching from an egg.

poison (POI son) poisonous — A substance that causes sickness or death when it enters the body.

prey (PREY) — An animal hunted or killed by another animal for food.

savannah (SA van nah) savannahs — Land covered with grass and a few trees.

venom (VEN om) — A chemical made in animals that makes other animals and people sick or kills them.

INDEX

Babies 16
Body 9, 16
Defense 20, 22
Eyes 11, 14
Fangs 14
Habitat 6
Jacobson's organ 11
Jaws 14
Length 9, 16
Movement 5, 6
Prey 11, 14, 19
Venom 14, 22
Weight 16
Windpipe 14